IMAGES
of America

WHITE SANDS
MISSILE RANGE

Judge—
For a true scholar
of history, not just
a "regurgitator of
facts."
Bennett
09 Jun 09

ONE OF THE PIONEERS OF EARLY ROCKETRY. Robert Goddard (left) is in his shop at Roswell, New Mexico. Goddard, along with German Hermann Oberth and Russian scientist Konstantin Tsiolkovsky, was instrumental in promoting the use of liquid-fueled rockets for space research and travel. On March 16, 1926, Goddard launched the first liquid-fueled rocket. Though it only reached an altitude of 41 feet, it demonstrated that this type of rocket could fly successfully. (White Sands Missile Range Museum.)

ON THE COVER: Preparations for a V-2 launch are ongoing as technicians make last-minute checks in this view inside the army blockhouse at Army Launch Area 1. All V-2s fired at the White Sands Proving Ground were launched from this control room. Today it is part of Launch Complex 33, a National Historical Landmark and New Mexico State Historical Monument. The gantry crane can also be found here. (White Sands Missile Range Museum.)

IMAGES
of America

WHITE SANDS
MISSILE RANGE

Darren Court and the
White Sands Missle Range Museum

ARCADIA
PUBLISHING

Published by Arcadia Publishing
Charleston SC, Chicago IL, Portsmouth NH, San Francisco CA

Printed in the United States of America

Library of Congress Catalog Card Number: 2008925024

For all general information contact Arcadia Publishing at:
Telephone 843-853-2070
Fax 843-853-0044
E-mail sales@arcadiapublishing.com
For customer service and orders:
Toll-Free 1-888-313-2665

Visit us on the Internet at www.arcadiapublishing.com

This book is dedicated to the men and women whose lives shaped the history contained within these pages—thank you all.

CONTENTS

ACKNOWLEDGMENTS

This book is a visual culmination of photographs showcased by many people who recognized the importance of preserving the history of the White Sands Missile Range (WSMR). Thomas Starkweather wrote detailed articles on the early history of the range. Maj. Gen. Niles J. Fulwyler (Ret.) was commanding officer at White Sands from 1982 to 1986, and his influence led to the restoration of the MacDonald Ranch House at the Trinity Site; he continues to be a staunch supporter of "Fort White Sands." The White Sands Historical Foundation and the White Sands Pioneer Group support the museum in tremendous aspects; Pam and Austin Vick, Dolores Archuleta, Jon Gibson, Pamela Hoscheid, David Soules, Francis Williams, and retired colonels Robert Lipinsky and Dan Duggan put forth a valiant effort to bring a new museum building into reality. The Public Affairs Office at White Sands has proven to be an invaluable resource, and I thank Monte, Lisa, and Cami for all of their support. Also thanks to Jim Eckles, who is retired from the Public Affairs Office and is a foundation member, for providing detailed information for this book. Terrie Cornell brought me back to White Sands after 13 years: I am grateful! And thanks go to Rebecca Balizan for helping with the photographs.

Thanks to Brig. Gen. Richard McCabe, commanding general of WSMR, and his wife, Maura; garrison commander Gary Giebel and his wife, Belinda; and Test Center director Bruce Lewis, Dennis Dekker, and the Morale, Welfare, and Recreation Directorate staff, who all have been strong supporters of the museum. The directorate provides the museum staff the resources available to fulfill its mission—to collect, preserve, interpret, and display the history of the Tularosa Basin, with an emphasis on military history. The main reason we can operate is our museum volunteers; without them, our doors would be closed, so a big thank-you to Doyle Piland, Joe Marlin, George Helfrich, Bill Jones, Glenn Moore, John Douds, Robert Watkins, Terry Chapell, and Fred and Debbie Walters. Their work can be seen at www.wsmr-history.org. All of the images in this book came from the White Sands Missile Range Museum, which were collected and preserved by those who have donated artifacts, photographs, and documents. Thank you all.

Now and forever, I thank my wife, Melissa, whose encouragement, especially during my frustrations, makes my efforts tangible, as well as my children, Dylan, Caitlyn, Meghan, and Kristen, who each provided comedic distractions when needed!

INTRODUCTION

White Sands Missile Range came into being with a Corps of Engineers Real Estate Directive issued on February 8, 1945, declaring that an area in the southern Tularosa Basin was of "military necessity;" the area met all of the requirements for a large, overland test range for rockets. These requirements included the range being within the continental United States, a large expanse of uninhabited area that would not impact any civilian population, surrounded by mountains or large hills that would be available for the installation of tracking instrumentation, good weather, and accessibility to transportation facilities. The area chosen was adjacent to both Fort Bliss and the Alamogordo Bombing Range, which later became Holloman Air Force Base, and close to Las Cruces and Alamogordo, New Mexico, as well as to El Paso, Texas. Much of the land chosen was already under government jurisdiction as part of Fort Bliss's Anti-Aircraft Firing Range, Dona Ana Target Range, and Castner Target Range, as well as the Alamogordo Bombing Range. Later agreements and permits allowed use of White Sands National Monument land, Jornada Experimental Range land, and other areas in the northern part of the range, which had previously been leased to ranchers for grazing allotments. The land that the Main Post occupies today was owned by the Cox family of San Augustine Ranch.

While decisions were being made for the development of White Sands, another event was taking place some 80 miles north of the White Sands Proving Ground cantonment area. Chosen largely for the same reasons as White Sands, the Trinity Site, in the northern Jornada del Muerto (or "Journey of Death"), had also been part of the Alamogordo Bombing Range. Trinity Base Camp was even bombed by a B-17 crew who mistook the camp for a target—nobody was hurt. Establishment of base camp began in the winter of 1944, and by the spring of 1945 (as the actual test of the "gadget," the atomic bomb, approached), it took on a feverish pitch. Engineers and scientists joined the military police who patrolled the area. One MP recalled playing volleyball with a net stretched from the barracks to the latrine, the games played with teams made up of enlisted soldiers and scientific notables such as Nobel Laureate Enrico Fermi.

The Trinity Site was the culmination of development and testing that had began in 1942, when U.S. president Franklin D. Roosevelt directed that research be conducted on the feasibility of beating the Germans to the atomic bomb. Roosevelt had been urged on by a letter sent to him, signed by Albert Einstein, stating that German scientists could potentially develop this new, powerful weapon. Under the direction of Gen. Leslie R. Groves, with scientific director J. Robert Oppenheimer, thousands had worked for years in Los Alamos, New Mexico; Hanford, Washington; Oak Ridge, Tennessee; and Wendover, Utah, in the development of the bomb—now it was time to test it. On July 16, 1945, the test was successful, and the world changed.

Exactly one week prior to the Trinity test, the first official flag raising at the new White Sands Proving Ground (WSPG) took place. Under the direction of its commanding officer, Lt. Col. Harold Turner, WSPG readied itself to accept captured V-2 parts and equipment, which had been removed from Germany at the end of World War II. The U.S. Army had already begun development of rockets and had used the area for testing under the ORDCIT program, begun the year before. In January 1944, the U.S. Army Ordnance Department requested that the Jet Propulsion Laboratory of the California Institute of Technology (CIT) begin investigating rockets similar to the V-2, and ORDCIT was born. The Private-A and Private-F rockets were the first developed out of this program, with the eventual development of the WAC Corporal.

While the WAC Corporal program was underway, V-2 rocket parts and materials had been arriving at the range, while contractors employed by General Electric and the Sperry Corporation worked with military and civilian scientists and engineers to evaluate the components and prepare to begin assembling them into complete rockets. Of the 117 German rocket scientists, led by Werner von Braun, who were brought to Fort Bliss to work on rocket development for the U.S. Army Ordnance Department, about 40 or so came north to work with the Americans at

WSPG. There were two purposes for firing the V-2 at White Sands, the first of which was to learn how to build, launch, and control large rockets. The second purpose was research. Numerous upper atmospheric experiments were conducted, including those for cosmic radiation, wind patterns, temperature, and biological experiments. A V-2 with a WAC Corporal mounted in the nose—Project Bumper—was the first two-stage liquid-fueled rocket to reach space. The first launch of a V-2 rocket occurred on April 16, 1946, and failed, falling back to the ground after only a 3.5-mile flight. Many who had worked on the rocket rushed out of the Army Blockhouse to view the launch, only to turn and try to run back in when the realization hit that the V-2 was coming down. The second flight, on May 10, 1946, was a success viewed by invited military officers, scientists, and the media. The American race for space had begun.

By the end of the V-2 program in 1951, a total of 67 V-2 rockets had been fired at White Sands. Under the Hermes Project, the army was interested in using other technologies developed by the Germans to develop large anti-aircraft missiles, as well as missiles that used ramjets and modified fins for gliding. Some of these programs were a success, and some were not, but all of the research and development taking place led to the development of the U.S. military's anti-aircraft, anti-missile, and artillery-type ground-to-ground missiles, some of which were nuclear capable. In addition, many of these technologies would be adapted for the National Aereonautics and Space Administration's (NASA) space programs. One such was the Redstone rocket, the generation following the V-2, designed by the German rocket team. In 1961, on two separate flights under the Mercury Project, Redstone boosters would put Alan Shepard and Gus Grissom into orbit. During the height of the cold war, White Sands Missile Range (renamed in 1958) became an invaluable asset to the country as weapons such as the Corporal, Lance, Pershing, Hawk, Chaparral, and Patriot were developed and tested. The army was not alone at White Sands, however.

By June 1946, the U.S. Navy had arrived, recognizing the role ballistic missiles would play in the fleet; White Sands was the perfect location to test. The Naval Research Laboratory (NRL) and Johns Hopkins University Applied Physics Lab (APL) were leaders of the V-2 research panel put together to develop research packages for V-2 flights. NRL also developed the Viking sounding rocket, with APL developing the Aerobee—rockets used for atmospheric research. The navy's Bumblebee Project was created toward the end of World War II in response to attacks by aircraft upon the fleet. Bumblebee led to the creation of the Talos, Terrier, and Tartar missiles, as well as the Typhon. Today the navy tests its standard missile on the range. The U.S. Air Force and NASA also conduct research and missile firings at White Sands, and many militaries from countries such as Germany, Japan, and South Korea make their way to the range for firing their weapon systems.

Throughout its existence, White Sands has been home to tens of thousands of single soldiers, military families, and civilians. Though isolated, the range has always provided an abundance of recreational activities for these soldiers and their families. Horseback riding has always been popular, and the stables, built in the 1950s, still remain in use. Clubs for military and civilian women have always played an important role in the range, giving women an opportunity to meet others, partake in classes and social events, and even travel in the area. Today these clubs support the range with scholarships and other important programs. Sports, as well, have always been a popular pastime, and the early WSPG teams often found themselves on the road, playing against other military teams and even some junior college squads. With its theater, enlisted and officers' clubs, community centers, outdoor recreation centers, and more, WSMR today continues to provide opportunities for recreation to those living on the post.

The photographs in this book, chosen to illustrate this remarkable history, all come from the archives of the White Sands Missile Range Museum. The archives are housed off-site from the museum and are run almost completely by volunteer labor. The Web site for the museum and archives is www.wsmr-history.org.

One

TRINITY SITE

TRINITY BASE CAMP. The camp was on the Jornada del Muerto, or Journey of Death, in 1945. Occupying part of what was then the Alamogordo Bombing Range, the site was chosen by test conductor Kenneth Bainbridge for the test of the first atomic bomb created under the Manhattan Project. The site met all of the requirements required by Gen. Leslie R. Groves and scientific director J. Robert Oppenheimer—it was at least 17-by-24 miles, in a relatively unpopulated area, and as close to Los Alamos as possible.

THE BASE CAMP MESS HALL. By November 1944, General Groves had signed a directive for constructing numerous barracks buildings, officers' quarters, latrine facilities, a commissary and supply warehouse, and this mess hall. The military police (MP) assigned to base camp supplemented their army food with pronghorn and deer shot with their service weapons, which Lt. Howard Bush, MP commander on the site, authorized.

THE MOTOR POOL, FALL OF 1945. By the fall of 1945, the Manhattan Project scientists had left, and most of the engineers had moved on. Only a small group of military police remained at base camp.

MILITARY POLICE (MP) SERGEANT MARVIN DAVIS. Davis was inducted on December 19, 1942, and received his MP training at Fort Riley, Kansas. Davis was one of the first MPs to arrive at Los Alamos, on April 19, 1943, and recalled that there were few people on "the Hill" at the time. His duties consisted of hauling furniture to the civilian houses, sawing wood, digging "ice out of the old Ice House," and patrolling the area with a nightstick. Many of the photographs seen here are from Davis's collection, which he donated to White Sands, along with some of his artifacts from the Trinity Site now in the WSMR Museum.

PFC ALEXANDER ALUKONIS AT POST No. 2. Most of the patrols of the site consisted of two men; however, guard posts themselves were manned by a single MP. This could cause problems, particularly if the guard had never been in the West before. One memorable moment found an MP asking how a "crawdad" could be so far from water. Davis was relieved to hear that the man had ignored it, as it was actually a scorpion.

11

LAZY MP RANCH. In a letter dated May 30, 1983, Marvin Davis recalled that this was "the building that we skidded from the old mine in Mockingbird Gap to be used as a blacksmith shop." This building was on the northwest side of base camp, near the stables and corrals that housed the MP company's horses. Saddle and tack were also housed here.

STABLE SERGEANT WILBUR "SHORTY" RUHLOW. This photograph shows the windmill and water cisterns for the horses in the background. The camp incorporated the old ranch houses of the Ross and Dave MacDonald families, so there were some troughs, wells, and windmills in existence prior to the camp building. For the most part, however, water had to be shipped in, as well as whiskey. By June 1945, adequate water was available.

LT. HOWARD C. BUSH ON HIS MARE, HONESTY. Marvin Davis wrote that he thought Bush was a captain when they were at base camp but that "most of the references" were of him as a lieutenant. Regardless, he "was a real diplomat, but he could get tough when he had to. He done everything he could to make things easier for everyone, military and civilians alike." Bush was liked and respected by all who met him at base camp.

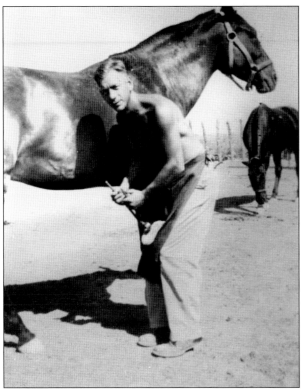

DICK COLEMAN AND SHORTY. Because of the nature of the terrain, the horses' hooves had to be constantly cared for; this photograph shows Coleman trimming one of Shorty's hooves. Davis states that they had 16 horses at Trinity, "re-mounts" from El Reno, Oklahoma, which were good compared to those they had been given in Los Alamos: they had a "rodeo checking those horses out. We had to rope them and tie them up short to saddle them up."

13

PREPARING FOR A RIDE. Since the military police were not using their horses for patrolling, they allowed the engineer company at base camp to use the horses, which they took on long rides around the area. Engineers had been brought to the camp for construction and included heavy equipment operators as well as cooks.

POLO AT BASE CAMP. One of the men's favorite pastimes was a match of polo. Lieutenant Bush would gather the men for polo games during down times, initially using soccer balls and broomsticks. Later Marvin Davis recalled, "I don't know how he got it, but he got some polo equipment for us, and we used to play out past the Motor Pool. We had the regulation helmets, mallets, and the wooden balls."

PREPARING FOR THE 100-TON TEST.
As the test of the actual atomic
bomb approached, the decision
was made to conduct a preliminary
test. One hundred tons of high
explosives were to be detonated along
with a small amount of fissionable
material so test procedures could be
checked and instruments calibrated.
A 20-foot-high wooden structure
was built to hold the explosives.

THE 100-TON TEST. This photograph
shows the stack of explosives on
the wooden tower just before it
was detonated. Though designed
to help calibrate the instruments
that would be used for the real
test in July, this May 7 test was
so powerful it actually destroyed
much of the instrumentation
and other experiments the
scientists had placed around it.

15

THE TOWER. During the summer of 1945, plans and construction reached a frantic pace. With the surrender of Germany, many scientists had begun to question continuing with the bomb; however, there was no discussion among the top scientific and military leadership about whether the development and test should continue. The 100-foot-tall metal tower for the shot was slowly going up by the middle of June 1945.

THE TOWER AT TRINITY SITE. The completed tower would house the "Gadget" for the first atomic bomb test. A wooden platform was built at the top with a removable floor, so the bomb could be winched up to the structure. There were two reasons for exploding the device in the air, one of which was the risk of fallout. A ground burst would have put immense amounts of contaminated soil into the air, and medical personnel on the project were already concerned about fallout clouds drifting over populated areas. Another reason was that the military wanted to have the actual devices explode just above their target, making the explosive force greater.

THE SOUTH 10,000-YARD BUNKER. The South 10,000-Yard Bunker was the control station for the Trinity test. Inside Lieutenant Bush kept watch over Oppenheimer, who was a mass of nerves by the time the test approached. Donald Hornig watched the clock to begin the countdown, with Joseph McKibben ready to start the firing sequence. This facility no longer exists.

TRINITY SITE TANK. One of two tanks on-site was used to enter the contaminated area after the explosion. The other tank broke down during preparations for the test, and this was the one used by Fermi to examine the blast pit of the bomb. Equipped with movable arms to recover soil samples, the vehicle became radioactive quite quickly and the men had to make a hasty escape.

JUMBO ON THE RAIL SIDING. Jumbo was a containment vessel—214 tons, 25 feet long, and a dozen feet in diameter, with 24-inch-thick steel walls—that had been built specifically for the testing of the bomb. It was feared that if the explosive lenses around the bomb failed to detonate the plutonium itself, it would be spread across the desert, making recovery difficult. Jumbo would contain the nuclear material should the explosion fail.

JUMBO AND A SPECIALLY BUILT TRAILER. Manhattan Project engineers had approached one of the nation's largest steel fabricators, but the company could not guarantee that it could build such a large container successfully, so Babcock and Wilcox Steel of Barberton, Ohio, fabricated it.

JUMBO IN EARLY SPRING OF 1945.
Because of Jumbo's size and weight, a
64-wheeled reinforced trailer was built
to carry it the 25 miles to the test site.
Tractors pulled the trailer, with Jumbo
arriving on-site on June 4, 1945.

LAS ALAMOS SCIENTISTS. By the
time of the test, Las Alamos scientists
had gained enough confidence in the
implosion design of the "Gadget" that
they felt Jumbo was unnecessary. It was
decided, instead, that a tower would be
built northwest of Ground Zero, with
Jumbo placed inside the tower. Jumbo
would be subjected to the blast from a
distance of about 800 yards.

UNSCATHED JUMBO. Jumbo survived the blast relatively unscathed; however, the same could not be said for the steel tower. The test conductor at Trinity, Kenneth Bainbridge, called Jumbo a "very weighty albatross around our necks." Later both ends would be blown out in an ill-conceived plan to destroy the vessel.

JUMBO TOURIST ATTRACTION. The decision not to use Jumbo as a containment vessel would prove wise, as it would have added an extra 214 tons of radioactive material to the atmosphere had it vaporized. Jumbo became a "tourist attraction" of sorts after the test, with many of the site's military and civilian workforce having their pictures taken with it. This continues today, as Jumbo remains at Trinity for visitors to see during one of the two open houses the range has each year.

THE GEORGE MCDONALD RANCH HOUSE. The master bedroom of the house had been converted into a clean room, with plastic taped over the windows and as much dust as possible removed from the room. On July 13, 1945, the two pieces of the core were assembled.

COOLING OFF. Military personnel take a swim in the cistern at the George McDonald ranch house. The ranch house, used for the final assembly of the "Gadget," had a divided water cistern and windmill to the east of the house. As the summer's heat increased during 1945, the cistern became a popular hangout.

THE CLEAN ROOM. The master bedroom of this 1,750-square-foot house was the dedicated clean room where the two halves of the bomb were to be assembled. Plastic was taped over the windows, and tables and benches were added. The two halves of the sphere were driven down to the Trinity Site on July 13, 1945, closely guarded by George Kistiakowsky, head of the Explosives Division at Los Alamos.

HEADING TO THE TOWER. During the afternoon of July 14, 1945, the now-assembled bomb was loaded into a sedan to be driven to the tower, where final assembly of the "Gadget" would take place.

TIME TO RAISE THE "GADGET." The bomb had been assembled and needed to be raised into the tower. Once it was being lifted, concerns were voiced regarding what would happen should the device fall. Mattresses and blankets were scavenged from base camp and were piled below the "Gadget" as it made its way into the tower.

LAST-MINUTE CHECK OF AN EXPERIMENT. Various experiments littered the site as the test date approached. Most of the materials used for the 100-ton test had been destroyed, so more had to be built and placed. These included such instruments as flash bombs, impulse meters, geophones, and peak pressure gauges.

DIRECTOR OF LOS ALAMOS. Norris Bradbury (left), who would succeed Oppenheimer as director of Los Alamos, is in the top of the tower examining the bomb. By this time, all of the various detonation timers and cables had been added, and the bomb was almost ready to go. Later that evening, a series of ferocious thunderstorms hit the area, with lightning crashing close to the tower. Inside the shelter on top, next to the bomb, sat Donald Hornig, babysitting the bomb and trying to read *Desert Island Decameron*, all the while hoping a stray bolt of electricity did not set off the bomb.

JULY 16, 1945, AT 5:49:45 A.M., THE WORLD CHANGED. By the time the bomb exploded, about 90 Los Alamos scientists were watching the explosion from about 20 miles away on Compania Hill. Among them were future Nobel winner Richard Feynman, as well as spy Klaus Fuchs, who would soon tell the Soviets what he had seen.

ONE OF THE TOWER FOOTINGS AFTER THE TEST. Because the "Gadget" was placed in a steel tower, there was a minimum of airborne fallout. Much of the soil and debris sucked up by the fireball condensed into droplets and fell as rain, forming a green glass-like substance called Trinitite. In addition to this material, only one of the tower footings remained and can still be seen today.

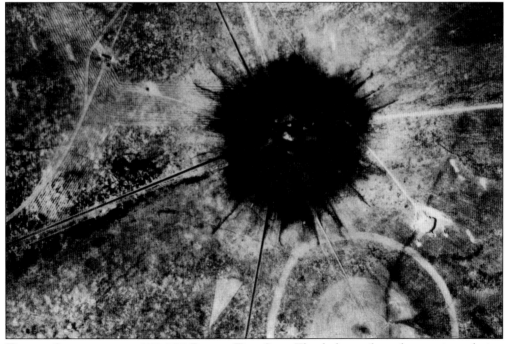

TRINITY SITE, WITH THE 100,000-POUND TEST SITE. The dark area from the atomic explosion consists of Trinitite. This was the view seen by George Cremeens when he broadcast his radio show from an airplane flying over Ground Zero in the fall of 1945. The Trinitite was later bulldozed apart and removed, though small pieces can still be seen.

RADIOMAN GEORGE CREMEENS WITH KENNETH BAINBRIDGE. In September 1945, George Cremeens (wearing striped shirt) of radio station KRNT, Des Moines, Iowa, was granted permission to travel to Ground Zero and record a series of four broadcasts. One of these was with Trinity test conductor Kenneth Bainbridge. It aired on Wednesday, September 26, 1945.

CREMEENS WITH CAPTAIN BUSH. Cremeens (wearing striped shirt) also interviewed the commanding officer of the military police detachment, Capt. Howard Bush (standing to Cremeens's left). Bush's interview aired on Thursday, September 17, 1945, and led to Cremeens corresponding with Captain Bush's mother, who eventually received a copy of the interview.

Two

WHITE SANDS
PROVING GROUND AND
THE V-2 PROGRAM

FLAG RAISING AT WHITE SANDS PROVING GROUND, JULY 9, 1945. This location, at the southern end of the Tularosa Basin, was chosen as the site where the army would assemble and fly the V-2 rocket captured in Germany toward the end of World War II. The area met Maj. Gen. Gladeon Barnes's requirements of good weather and open space along with accessibility to transportation and community services.

WHITE SANDS PROVING GROUND (WSPG). Harold Turner, first commanding officer of WSPG is seen at his desk in the headquarters building. Turner came to WSPG in July 1945 and quickly began building up the post, often using buildings scavenged from other locations, such as Fort Bliss, Texas, which almost led to his court-martial, as the post commander was unaware he had permission. The wooden V-2 rocket model on his desk was one of several he made and presented to visiting dignitaries. One can be seen today in the missile range's museum.

HAROLD TURNER IN FRONT OF THE HEADQUARTERS BUILDING. Turner was a master of public relations and sat for a number of radio and newspaper interviews. One of those who interviewed him was Virginia Strom of the *El Paso Times*. Strom eventually became Mrs. Harold Turner.

FOURTH OF JULY PARADE IN LAS CRUCES, NEW MEXICO. Harold Turner (standing third from left) is pictured at the 1946 Fourth of July parade in Las Cruces, New Mexico—the closest town to the post. Again, public relations were an important part of the early missile testing at WSPG, though Colonel Turner looks quite uncomfortable in his uniform standing in the July heat of the Chihuahuan desert.

THE ARMY BLOCKHOUSE. The Army Blockhouse is under construction at Army Launch Area 1 (ALA1). Construction of the blockhouse was begun the day after WSPG's birthday, on July 10, 1945. The blockhouse had walls of reinforced concrete 10 feet thick, with the roof having a thickness of 27 feet at its apex.

ALA1 Aerial View. The view is showing the isolation of the site in the southern Tularosa Basin. The Organ Mountains, in the background, provide a perfect buffer between missiles fired at WSPG and the city of Las Cruces. The blockhouse was designed and built to withstand a fully-loaded V-2 exploding 100 yards in front of it or falling onto it from an altitude of 100 miles.

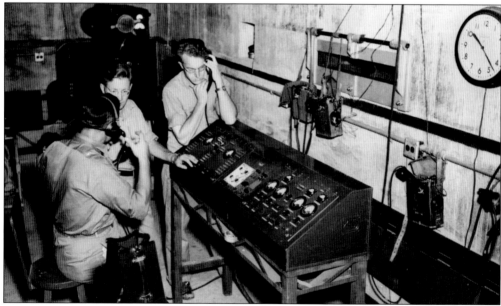

Interior of the Blockhouse, about 1946. This photograph of the blockhouse was taken quite a bit earlier than the cover photograph and probably shows the facility in early 1946. The firing commands were sent to the rocket by the console the three technicians are standing before. In contrast to the cover photograph, there is no telemetry equipment—the large cabinets against the wall on the cover—installed yet.

WSPG Aerial View, about 1946. This was the White Sands Proving Ground that the German rocket scientists would have seen upon their arrival in New Mexico. The missile assembly building is the large building in the foreground, with post headquarters immediately behind (north) of it. The white-roofed square buildings were the first enlisted quarters on the post and housed many of the early technicians who worked on the V-2. The roads in the right of the photograph went east, about six miles, out to Army Launch Area 1. Within a few years, most of these buildings would be replaced, and all that remains today is the first missile assembly building.

EARLY ENLISTED QUARTERS. These hutments were temporary but housed many of the early enlisted soldiers at WSPG. As the post population increased, a trailer park was added for enlisted married soldiers. By the early 1950s, permanent housing of cinder-block construction was built.

LAS CRUCES GATE. An early photograph shows the Las Cruces gate with enlisted member hutments. The wooden guard shack would not have provided much relief from the late summer sun and heat that characterizes the Tularosa Basin. The view is toward the west and shows San Andres Pass in the center of the photograph.

WSPG's First Gas Station. A caption attached to the photograph reads, "Early residents of White Sands Missile Range had a filling station for their convenience which, in 1948, was enlarged to two pumps. The facility was open two hours a day, Monday through Friday, and residents were encouraged to keep their cars near full in case of an emergency. Needless to say, residents were careful about unnecessary driving. Those who ran out of gas on Friday night were grounded until Monday."

V-2 Rockets Being Assembled in the Missile Assembly. By the fall of 1945, some 300 railroad cars of V-2 rocket parts and equipment had arrived in southern New Mexico. Colonel Turner requisitioned every flatbed truck in Dona Ana County, and it took 20 days to move all of the material over the pass from Las Cruces to WSPG. In addition, the German rocket scientists, led by Dr. Werner von Braun, had finally made their way to Fort Bliss, some 40 miles south of WSPG in El Paso, Texas.

DR. WERNER VON BRAUN. This giant of rocket research grew up in Berlin, once getting himself into trouble for firing a rocket-propelled wagon down a busy street. Though he had a passing interest in space, it was not until he received a copy of Hermann Oberth's *The Rocket Into Interplanetary Space* that he became serious about physics and mathematics. By the 1930s, he was a member of a German rocket enthusiasts group and worked for Oberth firing small rockets. He soon began working with German artillery captain Walter Dornberger on rocket research. By the early 1940s, an extensive research and production facility for rockets had been built at Peenemunde, on Germany's Baltic Coast; now-general Dornberger was military commander, with von Braun as scientific director. Peenemunde was the birthplace of the V-2 rocket, developed as a weapon and fired against targets such as London and Antwerp. At the end of the war, many members of the German rocket team, including von Braun, surrendered to the United States. They eventually made their way to Fort Bliss, Texas, and White Sands Proving Ground, where they helped the U.S. Army assemble captured V-2s and build new ones.

ASSEMBLY OF PIPING ON THE COMBUSTION CHAMBER. The complex combustion system of the V-2 rocket was the result of many failed designs and tests. The system utilized a fuel of alcohol and water, with a liquid oxygen oxidizer. The fuels were driven into the combustion chamber through the use of a hydrogen peroxide–driven pump.

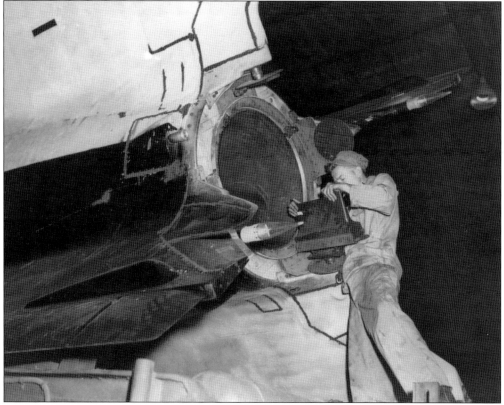

ATTACHING THE CARBON VANES. The V-2 rocket had two methods of steering. For flight within the atmosphere, the rocket could be steered with the fins. However, once the rocket was in the upper atmosphere or in near space, carbon vanes placed in the engine exhaust were used to steer the rocket. The vanes were one of the last items assembled and were made of carbon. Clyde Tombaugh found it easy to follow V-2 rockets in the upper atmosphere by watching the carbon vanes, which turned a bright orange from the rocket exhaust.

FORWARD HATCH OPEN. The first two flights of the V-2 at WSPG were made using a modified German warhead. As scientific packages became larger and more complicated, a modified "warhead," or nose cone, was developed, which had numerous access panels so test instrumentation could be easily uninstalled and modified.

READY FOR A STATIC TEST. This photograph shows a partially assembled V-2 ready for static testing. Note that the rear fin section has not been assembled. This "partial" rocket would be trucked a few miles south of the missile assembly building to a test stand built into the side of a hill.

A 50,000 STATIC TEST STAND WITH V-2 ERECTED. The V-2 would be erected in a steel gantry to test fire the engines, checking for any problem that would affect the flight of the missile or contribute to its failure.

V-2 FIRING ON THE TEST STAND. During one of the first test firings at the Static Test Stand, the heat of the rocket motor caused steel plates to buckle and fail. It also caused a fire in the desert brush almost 250 yards from where the rocket was fired.

V-2 BEING LOADED ON A MEILERWAGEN. The Meilerwagen was of German design and was used at White Sands to transport the V-2 out to the launch area and erect it on the Brennstand, or firing platform. Prior to the building of the gantry crane, it also provided access to the top of the erected rocket.

V-2 BEING SECURED TO MEILERWAGEN, READY TO GO. The truck in the foreground of this photograph is of particular importance, as it belongs to the 9393 Technical Support Unit (TSU). These "Broomstick Scientists" were drafted into the army and sent to work with the Hermes program at WSPG. They contributed to the success of the V-2, Corporal, and Nike Ajax programs.

LEAVING THE TECH AREA. This photograph and the next 10 depict various activities in support of V-2 shot number two. The first V-2 shot at WSPG, on April 16, 1946, only managed to reach an altitude of 3.5 miles before coming back down a mile from the blockhouse. The second shot, on May 10, 1946, was successful.

HEADING TO ARMY LAUNCH AREA 1. By this point, the rocket had been checked out and was almost ready to go. After leaving the technical area, the V-2s were driven about 6 miles east of the main post area to be erected and fired from the Army Blockhouse.

AT ARMY LAUNCH AREA 1, A V-2 ERECTED FOR FIRING. The rocket has arrived at the launch site and is in the process of being erected for firing. Once erected, it will be fueled, and final checks will be made of the instrumentation package on-board.

ERECTED V-2 AT ARMY LAUNCH AREA 1. By now, the rocket firing stand would have been raised to contact the fins at the base of the rocket, and one of the clamping collars is shown unconnected. A second ladder trailer is being moved up to the rocket. The WAC Corporal missile tower is on the right.

FINAL INSTRUMENT ADJUSTMENTS. V-2 round number two carried a variety of instruments that needed to be checked out prior to the rocket's launch. There were instruments to measure cosmic radiation, as well as cameras for high-altitude photography. The modified German warhead shown here would no longer be used after this flight.

LOADING ALCOHOL ABOARD V-2 PREPARATORY TO LAUNCHING. The V-2 used a mixed ethyl alcohol (75 percent) and water (25 percent) fuel with a liquid oxygen oxidizer to deliver 55,000 pounds of thrust at take-off. The fuels were delivered to the combustion chamber by a steam-driven pump.

FUELING V-2 WITH HYDROGEN PEROXIDE. The turbo pump was driven by steam generated by combining hydrogen peroxide and sodium permagnate. This steam drove the turbines, which forced the fuel into the combustion chamber.

MAJ. HERB KARSCH ON V-2 FIRING PLATFORM. Karsch was a member of the team that brought the German rocket scientists to the United States under Operation Paperclip. He arrived at White Sands in June 1945 as the Ordnance Technical Intelligence Officer and left the range in 1956. He is a member of the White Sands Hall of Fame.

COL. HAROLD TURNER INSPECTS THE V-2. Colonel Turner looks over V-2 shot number two before its firing. For the second V-2 shot, Turner invited many dignitaries, as well as the press, to White Sands to view the firing. On May 27, 1946, *Life* magazine ran a story on this particular V-2 shot.

VISITING DIGNITARIES. From left to right are British field marshal Sir Henry Maitland Wilson, Adm. DeWitt Ramsey, Col. Harold Turner, and Gen. Joe Stillwell. Even though the first V-2 shot at White Sands was considered a failure, Colonel Turner still felt the second shot was a go. Therefore, in addition to the media and other dignitaries invited, military notables also made their way to White Sands to view the second launch.

OVERVIEW OF PREPARATIONS FOR FIRING. The WAC Corporal tower is at right. A spectacular photograph of the launch area, support equipment, and vehicles, this image shows the liquid oxygen fueling trailer in front of the V-2.

V-2 ROCKET NUMBER 21 AFTER BEING ERECTED. By the time round 21 was fired, engineers had mainly succeeded in developing a way to separate the rocket into pieces so the instrumentation packages could be recovered. A series of small explosions were detonated at the base of the warhead section, causing it to separate and come down.

VIEW FROM SPACE. The first photographs and film showing the earth's curvature from space were taken by V-2 rockets at White Sands Proving Ground. The first of these, taken on October 24, 1946, from an altitude of about 65 miles, showed some 40,000 square miles of the earth's surface. The warhead section separated at 25 miles as the rocket descended. The camera was destroyed, but the film remained intact.

ANOTHER V-2, INSTRUMENTATION BEING CHECKED. The German warhead was too heavy for instrumentation and did not allow accessibility. The Naval Research Laboratory developed a lighter-weight warhead that provided about 20 cubic feet for instrumentation. The warheads varied depending upon the type of instrumentation required.

SHOT NUMBER 25 BEING ERECTED.
The Meilerwagen has backed up to the firing stand, and the rocket is ready to be erected. The firing stand provided not only a platform for firing the rocket, but also allowed for the connection of cabling and fueling hoses.

FUELING V-2 NUMBER 25, ERECTED IN THE GANTRY CRANE. Construction of the gantry crane began in August 1946; by November, it was completed. The crane was built to service missiles up to a height of 54 feet. First used for the V-2, it was also used for the various Hermes missiles, as well as the Corporal.

V-2 Number 25—The Gantry Crane. The crane was rolled into place around the rocket after it was erected on the launch table. After servicing, it then rode on a set of railroad tracks away from the launch area.

V-2 Preparations. The launch of a V-2 was always a special event at White Sands. Scientists and engineers who had designed the experiments or developed the on-board instrumentation, as well as those fueling the rocket and performing other servicing missions, ensured that Army Launch Area 1 was a busy place as the launch date approached.

TRAINING FLIGHT 3. By June 1951, General Electric's participation in the V-2 program came to an end, with all V-2 operation transferring to U.S. Army ordnance. Nine static tests of the propulsion units were made, and five upper-atmosphere shots had been made by the end of September 1952. These were called "training flights."

TRAINING FLIGHT 3 IN THE GANTRY CRANE. A nighttime view shows Training Flight 3 in the gantry crane, with final preparations ongoing. Training Flight 3 was the first V-2 to be completely assembled, tested, and fired by military personnel—the "Broomstick Scientists." One training flight missile reached an altitude of 132 miles, the highest of any V-2 fired during the program.

LAUNCH AT ALA1. A view of the launch includes the gantry crane and WAC Corporal tower to the right. A heavily modified warhead can be seen on this rocket. Some warhead instrumentation had to be pressurized, shielded, or somehow protected against flight effects. When enough instrumentation could not be added to bring the weight of the warhead up to 2,000 pounds—the weight of the original German warhead—lead weights were added.

BLOSSOM PROJECT. Shot number 47 leaves the ground in front of the blockhouse on June 6, 1949. A particularly interesting shot, number 47 was part of the "Blossom Project," in which parachute recovery systems were developed to bring the warhead back to the ground. Five of the Blossom shots also carried live animals into space to investigate the potential dangers and limitations of space flight. V-2 rocket number 47 carried Albert II, a rhesus monkey, into the sky, and respiratory and cardio data were recovered. Albert II, unfortunately, was not, as his parachute failed to deploy.

BUMPER SHOT 5. The Bumper Project was the army's attempt to develop a two-stage rocket, using the V-2 as the booster for the WAC Corporal. The first six, of eight total, Bumper shots were fired at White Sands. Bumper 5 set an altitude record, with the WAC Corporal reaching a height of 244 miles.

FUEL TANKS EXPLODE. Not all shots were a success. In this photograph, one of the fuel tanks explodes as the result of the explosives used to separate the warhead prematurely detonating. The explosive detonation cord was supposed to blow the warhead from the rocket upon descent; however, in this shot, flight initiation detonated the cord, which blew the fuel tanks as well.

MISSILE MISHAP. The undated photograph is probably of a V-2 launch where the rocket failed to develop sufficient thrust for liftoff. The rocket rose less than a foot off the firing table, then slowly skittered to the side before tilting over and exploding.

ARMY BLOCKHOUSE AND THE ORGAN MOUNTAINS. All that is recognizable in this photograph is the bottom fin section of the rocket. It shows the Army Blockhouse and the Organ Mountains to the west. This is the result of another short circuit, which caused the separation explosives to detonate prematurely.

V-2 Impact Crater up Range. The combustion chamber can be seen in the bottom of the crater. Although the V-2s fired at White Sands did not carry explosives, the kinetic energy of the rocket, combined with the explosion of residual fuels, caused immense impact craters when the rocket came down.

The Result of a Successful V-2 Launch—Debris in the Desert. This is a V-2 thrust frame lying in the desert after a successful test. By the end of the program, 67 V-2s had been launched at White Sands, giving the military and scientists important new data unobtainable from other sources.

Three

WHITE SANDS PROVING GROUND ENTERS A NEW ERA

VIKING ROCKET IN THE GANTRY CRANE.
A Viking rocket in the gantry crane,
round number six, was ready to fire on
December 11, 1950. The Viking program
was a high-altitude sounding rocket program
proposed by the Naval Research Laboratory
in 1949. The rocket could carry a payload of
100 pounds to an altitude of 158 miles.

STATIC FIRING OF VIKING ROUND 9. There were 11 Vikings built and fired using the same alcohol and liquid oxygen fuel system as the V-2. Built by the Glenn L. Martin Company, the first Viking was fired at White Sands on May 3, 1949, reaching an altitude of 50 miles before premature engine cut-off. Like most rockets developed at the time, static tests were conducted to ensure the propulsion systems were ready.

VIKING ROUND NUMBER NINE. After the Viking round number nine was static fired, it was loaded with fuel and launched. This particular Viking reached more than 130 miles high. The Naval Research Laboratory's success with the Viking led to the Vanguard program, intended to launch the first artificial satellite into orbit.

CORPORAL MISSILE ON ITS TRANSPORTER/ERECTOR, ABOUT 1951. The Corporal program was America's first designed, engineered, and fabricated surface-to-surface missile and the first U.S. guided missile to be approved for nuclear armament. It drew upon the experience gained from the German rocket team.

PREPARING TO ERECT CORPORAL ROUND 11, AUGUST 3, 1951. Corporal's immediate forerunner was the Corporal E test vehicle, a WAC Corporal redesigned for increased performance, decreased weight, and easier production. Corporal E first flew in May 1947 to evaluate basic guided-missile principles. In 1950, the decision was made to develop it further into Corporal.

CORPORAL ROUND 7 ERECTED ON LAUNCHER, JANUARY 16, 1951. Corporal was launched by a rocket motor using liquid red fuming nitric acid as the oxidizer. In 1955, the first Corporal battalion, the 259th and the 96th Direct Support unit, was the first U.S. missile unit to be deployed overseas. The Corporal was replaced by the Sergeant by 1964.

HERMES A-1 MISSILE ERECTED FOR FIRING, MAY 19, 1950. The Hermes A-1 was the American version of the German Wasserfall, an anti-aircraft rocket developed by the Germans during the war. The project had begun in 1946, the same year the Nike project started up and was soon relegated to a research role, testing guidance and control systems.

HERMES A-1 ROUND NUMBER FIVE, MARCH 14, 1951. In May 1950, and again in September, launches of the Hermes 1-A were not successful. The first actual flight of this rocket occurred in February 1951, and the program was soon discontinued because flight after flight was cut short because of technical problems.

HERMES 2 ON LAUNCH TABLE. Popular lore refers to a V-2 rocket that flew the wrong way, heading south instead of north and landing in or near a cemetery south of Juarez, Mexico. Ernst Steinhoff, in charge of guidance for the rocket, let it go rather than destroying it over El Paso, Texas, in the hope that it would clear both El Paso and Juarez, Mexico, just across the Rio Grande—his chance paid off. However, the rocket was not a V-2; it was actually a Hermes II. This rocket was developed to test new ramjet technologies and was one of the most secret projects at White Sands at the time; it was much easier to say it was a V-2.

AEROBEE LAUNCH, JUNE 7, 1951.
The Aerobee became the U.S.
Navy's workhorse for its sounding
rocket program in part because of
its 150-pound payload capacity.
First fired in 1947, Aerobee would
stay in use until the last round
was launched at White Sands
on January 17, 1985. This early
shot depicts Aerobee 19 leaving
its launch tower. Aerobee would
be the first research rocket to
reach 200 miles in altitude.

HONEST JOHN LAUNCH, FEBRUARY 11, 1952. Honest John was a non-guided, free-flight rocket that carried a nuclear punch. Development began in 1950, with flight testing the following year. By January 1954, the first rockets were deployed with units in Europe. Beginning in 1973, Lance missiles began to replace Honest Johns.

REDSTONE FUELING. A Redstone is fueling with a fire truck standing by. Redstone was the army's largest surface-to-surface ballistic missile. Modified Redstone rockets launched America's first satellite and first human into space. Developed by von Braun and his team, it was a direct descendant of the V-2.

REDSTONE ROCKET AND THE REDSTONE GANTRY. As a field artillery missile, Redstone was designed to extend the firepower and range of conventional artillery against ground targets: it could deliver a nuclear of high-explosive warhead to targets 200 miles away. Since it was a ballistic missile, its inertial trajectory and guidance was provided by the launcher. Great care was taken to level the missile and to orient the stabilized platform accurately in the direction of the target.

REDSTONE LAUNCH. Redstone's liquid fuel engine burned alcohol and liquid oxygen, producing about 75,000 pounds of thrust. As a field artillery missile, Redstone was mobile and transportable by airplane, truck, or train. However, on the move, it needed a convoy 18 miles long, with 200 vehicles carrying about 10,000 individual pieces of equipment and more than 600 troops. The rocket itself was carried on three trucks—its nose section (warhead), midsection (power plant and fuel tanks), and tail section—to be assembled in the field.

WSPG OPEN HOUSE, MAY 1959. The large rocket in the foreground is the Redstone. Other rockets and missiles include the Talos, Lacrosse, Nike Hercules, and Corporal. These open houses were an opportunity to share with the public the research and development occurring at the range.

THE 500,000-POUND STATIC TEST FACILITY. Built on the northeastern flank of the Organ Mountains, the facility was designed as a static test facility for rocket motors having up to a half million pounds of thrust. The largest rocket ever tested here was the Redstone.

STATIC TEST OF REDSTONE MOTOR NUMBER TWO, NOVEMBER 8, 1951. Static testing was crucial to large rockets like the Redstone. It gave missile crews and technicians a chance to test new modifications to the thrust systems without the danger of a rocket failing in flight.

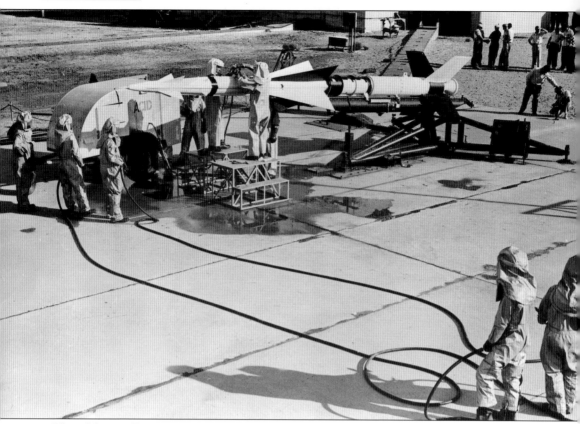

NIKE MISSILE ROUND 66, OCTOBER 15, 1951. The Nike program was designed as America's first line of defense against Soviet bombers. Ajax was a two-stage liquid-fueled missile with a solid-propellant booster. The sustainer motor used red fuming nitric acid and JP-4 fuel to produce 2,600 pounds of thrust for 30 seconds. It delivered high-explosive warheads to a radar-determined intercept point with target aircraft. Nike Ajax was deployed by 1953, with the first firing battery at Fort Meade, Maryland. By 1962, two hundred forty additional launch sites were developed.

NIKE AJAX READY FOR LAUNCH, APRIL 24, 1952. The Nike Ajax made history because it was armed for the first time with a live warhead; the Nike Ajax missile successfully intercepted and destroyed in mid-air a remotely controlled QB-17 bomber high over White Sands Proving Ground. A three-man tracking crew photographed the moment of intercept. Their photograph won the 1955 Ernie Pyle Award for outstanding contribution toward national security by a still photograph. The award can be seen in the WSMR museum.

HEADQUARTERS OF RED CANYON RANGE CAMP (RCRC), 1956. Lying in the northeastern part of the range, RCRC was where the U.S. Army's Nike crews fired missiles during their Annual Service Practices (ASPs). Nike crews from all over the country came to RCRC once a year to fire their missiles against target drone aircraft.

RCRC POST EXCHANGE (PX). The caption on the reverse of this November 9, 1956, photograph reads, "This is a Butler Constructed Type Building, 40 x 80 feet. The best building in the camp, but not large enough to accommodate the business the PX does at this camp, $150,000 a year sales."

RECREATION CENTER READING ROOM AT RCRC. The caption on the reverse of this February 26, 1957, image reads, "Library of Service Club at Red Canyon Range Camp being used by personnel." With the nearest town many miles away, there was little for the men at the camp to do during the week; however, almost without exception, the men of RCRC to this day consider it one of the best tours of duty they ever had.

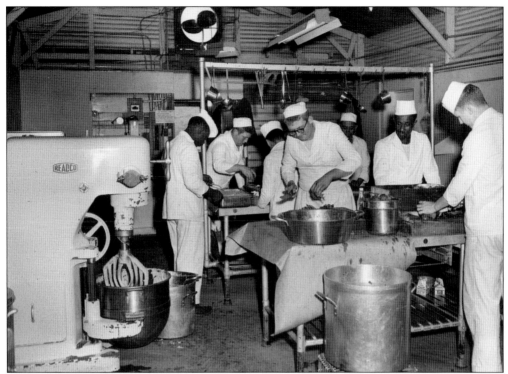

MESS HALL KITCHEN AT RCRC. The caption on the back of this November 9, 1956, photograph reads, "Mess Hall, depicting size of this 21' x 51' kitchen which is a tight squeeze for the 10 cooks who prepare meals daily. In this capsuled area cooking, baking, butchering for the 3600 fed daily is done. There is need for additional equipment but presently there is no additional space to accommodate more. Water is piped from a tank on a hill above the mess hall, but in the winter it freezes."

GEN. WILLARD WYMAN. Wyman, the commanding general of CONARC (Continental Army Command), far right, talks to the medical officer (far left) at Red Canyon Range Camp on May 27, 1958. RCRC was in the public eye during its existence and attracted not only high-ranking military officers, such as General Wyman, but also many foreign dignitaries and officials from many cities across the nation who came to see what the troops stationed in their cities did with the Nike Ajax.

OFFICERS' SHOWERS AT RCRC. Shown on November 9, 1956, the facility consisted of two 1942 surplus 8-by-16-foot trailers. Inside were four small shower stalls and two sinks. This facility accommodated 125 officers daily.

ENLISTED WASH AREA, NOVEMBER 9, 1956. The caption on the reverse reads, "Shower and washroom, 42 shower stalls to accommodate 1100 permanent enlisted members. Heated by two tiny oil stoves whose effectiveness is practically nil in the cold weather of the range. Building is made of salvaged material and is damp and of little shelter from weather."

MESS HALL WASH AREA, NOVEMBER 9, 1956. "All cooking utensils and trays are washed in this small building consisting of two salvaged 16' x 16' huts," reads the original caption to this image. "Water is heated by immersion heaters and carried into the wash-house and poured into the sinks. Wash water is drained into a sump which was built by unit troops."

SINGLE OFFICERS' QUARTERS AT RCRC. These salvaged trailers, shown on February 14, 1956, were covered with tar paper in an attempt to insulate them and try to keep out the fine dust and dirt, which would often accompany dry thunderstorms in the area. The sandbags around them were an attempt to keep out storm waters.

Gen. Willard Wyman and Capt. Milo D. Rewall. Here is General Wyman again, on May 27, 1958. Here General Wyman talks to D Battery, 55st BN commander Capt. Milo D. Rewall. Looking on are Sp2c. Ernest H. Moore, Cpl. Robert E. Hathcock, Pvt. James E. Maraden, and Sp3c. Robert J. Whitener.

The Chapel at RCRC. The chapel at RCRC was built with all-volunteer labor using scrap and salvaged materials during the winter of 1957–1958. The pillars at the front of the church are actually telephone poles covered in mortar to resemble stone, and the frame of the building was built out of disused railroad tracks. The chapel was the brainchild of RCRC commanding officer Lt. Col. John McCarthy and MSgt. William Sidell, who drew up the plans.

CHAPEL WALLS. This photograph shows the chapel walls. The wood for the siding, flooring, and roof came from salvaged Nike Ajax missile crates, with the men donating about $200, which was used to buy shingles for the roof.

CHAPEL UNDER CONSTRUCTION. Volunteers are hammering the trim onto the chapel. The stone used for the exterior of the chapel was quarried by volunteers from a hillside not far from RCRC, and windows were given a stained-glass effect by the use of shellac and colored cellophane paper.

MSGT. WILLIAM SIDELL. MSgt. William Sidell (left) supervises the addition of the steeple. This took several tries thanks to a strong wind that came up just as the men began to hoist the steeple over the chapel.

CHAPEL DEDICATION. The army's chief of chaplains, Maj. Gen. Patrick Ryan, dedicated the partially completed chapel on January 22, 1958, during a visit to nearby Fort Bliss, Texas. He stated, "A building such as this means more than a large and expensive chapel built by congressional appropriation. This has the heart and soul of you men in it."

CHAPEL INTERIOR. The interior of the completed chapel included a handmade alter and cross. One hundred and three volunteers from 33 states and the Philippines took part in the construction of the chapel. The first service was held on Easter in 1958. Protestant services were held each Sunday morning and Monday evening, with a priest from nearby Carrizozo, New Mexico, holding Catholic Mass on Sunday afternoon. The chapel, one of the last buildings remaining when RCRC closed, was eventually dismantled, leaving only its foundation.

HON. MARY V. BECK. This photograph, dated January 28, 1959, shows the Honorable Mary V. Beck (center), president of the Detroit Common Council, and Mrs. S. L. A. Marshall (right), wife of military historian S. L. A. Marshall, waiting on VIP Hill during a firing at RCRC. They were just a few of the thousands of dignitaries, from many states and nations, who visited RCRC.

LAUNCHING THE 12,000TH MQM-33, RCAT DRONE AT RCRC. The RCAT (Radio-Controlled Aerial Target) Drone was the workhorse for the Nike Ajax and firing batteries at Red Canyon Range Camp. About 200 RCATs a week were flown from the RCAT Firing Battery's camp at Oscura. RCATs were phased out of the army by the mid-1960s.

BRIGHT EYES. The first tracking telescope-camera was built at White Sands by Clyde Tombaugh. Tombaugh, who had discovered the planet Pluto in 1930, came to White Sands in 1946. The first successful track of a V-2 rocket was made with this camera-telescope assembly built on a World War II M-45 gun mount. The film revealed that, as the rocket fuel burned out, it caused the rocket to wobble, seriously degrading its performance.

INTERCEPT GROUND OPTICAL RECORDER (IGOR). The IGOR is a tracking telescope designed to provide photographic records of missile performance, such as altitude, intercept miss distance, and other event data; it could photograph targets up to 100 miles away.

STILL CAMERAS SET UP TO CAPTURE A LAUNCH. Every launch at White Sands was photographed extensively, often from several angles. The purpose of these still photographs was to record exactly what the rocket or missile was doing at a particular point in time.

BOWEN-KNAPP PHOTOGRAPH RECORDER. One of many of the optical devices used to film rockets and missile at White Sands, these recorders have been used in many of the tests and were part of the photo-optical shot developed by Clyde Tombaugh to record flight data.

ASKANIA PHOTOGRAPH RECORDING THEODOLITE. These instruments were used to track and record missiles in flight. About 50 to 60 of these were used in the integrated range concept, and they recorded azimuth and elevation data synchronized with time.

MITCHELL PHOTOGRAPH RECORDING THEODOLITE. These were used in addition to the Askania systems, but there were far fewer of them in place during the early years of the range.

LIEUTENANT CONDRON, NAMESAKE OF CONDRON FIELD. Max Henderson Condron, from Valley, Nebraska, entered the service on October 30, 1941. He received his army pilot's training at Garner Field in Uvalde, Texas; Perrin Field in Sherman, Texas; and Brooks Field in San Antonio, Texas.

CONDRON FIELD IN 1956. Commissioned a second lieutenant on April 16, 1942, Condron was stationed at Fort Sill, Oklahoma, and Fort Riley, Kansas, before being sent to the 6th Tow Target Squadron at Biggs Field in El Paso, Texas. He was killed on December 3, 1942, at the age of 21, on a Flying Search Light Mission.

CONDRON FLYING CLUB. Workers are pushing an airplane into a maintenance shop. At least until the late 1990s, Condron Field typically had about four flights a day, though during exercises this could increase to more than 40. The field is still in use today.

Four

THE MISSLES OF WHITE SANDS

NORTHWEST END OF THE TECH AREA, ABOUT 1960. Soldiers and civilian technicians are pictured at the northwest end of the tech area. The following missiles are seen, clockwise from front left: Little John, Nike Ajax, Nike Hercules, Lacrosse, Corporal, Honest John, Talos, Hawk, and Dart.

NIKE HERCULES BEING PREPARED FOR LAUNCH, 1966. The Nike Hercules was the U.S. Army's only deployed nuclear-armed surface-to-air weapon. Its mission was air defense of major urban centers against enemy bombers. Later this mission was changed to defense against enemy missiles rather than bombers.

NIKE HERCULES LAUNCH, NOVEMBER 10, 1964. Developed as a replacement for the Nike Ajax, the Hercules was essentially an Ajax with four of each component: a cluster of four solid-fuel rocket boosters to accelerate the missile and four liquid-propellant engines to carry the warhead to the target.

NIKE HERCULES SHOT, JULY 13, 1966. During the cold war, the U.S. Army established 145 Nike Hercules sites in the continental United States, protecting metropolitan areas and Strategic Air Command sites. They remained deployed until 1974; abroad they were in service until the 1990s. More than 25,000 Hercules missiles were manufactured during its history, with 680 being fired at White Sands.

NIKE ZEUS. According to the caption attached to this photograph, dated November 7, 1961, "Standard preliminary procedures must be followed for loading Nike Zeus on the research and development launcher at Army Launch Area 5, White Sands Missile Range, NM. Missile is placed in elevated position to finish check out." The Nike Zeus was developed as a replacement for the Nike Hercules.

NIKE ZEUS ERECTED AND READY FOR LAUNCH. This photograph is of the Nike Zeus B, a much better, more reliable, and more capable version than the A. It had an extended range and was designed to kill re-entry vehicles before they entered the atmosphere.

SPRINT MISSILE LAUNCH FROM LAUNCH COMPLEX 50. The Sprint Missile project was designed to be part of the Sentinel program, later downsized to become Safeguard. Sentinel was an anti-ballistic missile system developed to protect American cities from nuclear attack. Safeguard, developed in the 1960s, was designed to protect U.S. Intercontinental Ballistic Missile (ICBM) sites.

SPRINT MISSILE TURNING, DOWN-RANGE TRAJECTORY, MAY 3, 1966. The Sprint Missile was an amazing bit of engineering, able to reach speeds of Mach 10 within 5 seconds of launch. It was a solid-fuel anti-ballistic missile that carried a W66 enhanced radiation thermonuclear warhead designed to destroy the target by the use of neutron flux.

HAWK MISSILE LAUNCHER, 1963. "Hawk Missile Project: Checking missile launcher at Army Launch Area No. 2, WSMR, NM 26 FEB 63. SGT Keith Yankers and SSG J.R. Searey," reads the original caption on this image. Development of the HAWK (Homing All the Way Killer) began in 1952, and it entered service in 1960.

HAWK MISSILE LAUNCH FROM LAUNCH COMPLEX 32. The Hawk was unique for its time in that it used an active homing guidance, which could engage targets at low altitudes, disregarding the ground clutter in the background while tracking a target.

CHAPARRAL MISSILE BEING LOADED, NOVEMBER 2, 1983. The Chaparral was a short-range air defense missile system. The missile was a modified Sidewinder, with the launcher carrying four missiles loaded, with eight more in special missile "coffins" inside the tracked vehicle.

CHAPARRAL MISSILE LAUNCH. The launcher can be seen clearly here. The gunner sat in a turret erected 21 inches from the base of the vehicle. The Chaparral vehicle consisted of the launcher itself and the tracked vehicle that carried it. The launcher could be removed from the tracked vehicle for air mobility, being sling-loaded beneath a helicopter and transported where needed.

STINGER MISSILE LAUNCH. One of the MANPADS (Man-Portable Air Defense Systems), the Stinger was a shoulder-fired missile effective against aircraft. During the 1980s, Stinger missiles made their way to Afghanistan and were used successfully by the Muhadjedin in their war against the Soviet Union.

PATRIOT MISSILE LAUNCH AT LAUNCH COMPLEX 33. The Patriot is a long-range, all-weather, air defense missile designed initially to replace the Nike Hercules and the Improved Hawk. It is the only operational air defense system that can target both aircraft and missiles.

PATRIOT MISSILE LAUNCH. Patriot planning began in October 1964 as a defense against aircraft but was slowed by the requirement that the new system should use a track-via-missile guidance. Testing at White Sands finally began in 1970; the first combat use of the Patriot occurred during Operation Desert Storm in 1991.

HONEST JOHN MISSILE LEAVING ITS LAUNCHER, JUNE 10, 1982. Even after almost 40 years, this missile was still being deployed. By 1973, it had been replaced by the Lance missile, and Honest Johns were then transferred to the U.S. Army National Guard, remaining in service until the early 1980s.

SERGEANT MISSILE ON LAUNCHER, MARCH 12, 1964. The Sergeant missile was developed as an artillery-type weapon, the first solid-fuel ground-to-ground weapon deployed by the U.S. Army. It could carry a high explosive or nuclear warhead.

SERGEANT MISSILE LAUNCH. The Sergeant program officially began in 1955, with the first firing at White Sands the following year. The missile was deployed in 1956, and a complete system could be moved with much less effort than the Corporal, which it was designed to replace. After a launch site had been reached, the missile could be launched in less than an hour.

PREPARATIONS FOR PERSHING MISSILE LAUNCH. The Pershing was the first and only solid-fueled Medium-Range Ballistic Missile (MRBM) deployed by the U.S. Army; it replaced the Redstone. Development of the Pershing was quick. Initial feasibility studies began in late 1956, and on February 25, 1960, the first Pershing was launched.

PERSHING ERECTED FOR LAUNCH. The Pershing was a two-stage solid-fueled rocket with an all-inertial guidance system fired from a mobile launcher. With this transporter-erector-launcher, the missile operated on a "shoot and scoot" principle. It was both ground and air transportable, nuclear capable, and featured a high-speed re-entry vehicle.

LAUNCH OF A PERSHING II MISSILE. The Pershing II was an improved version of the Pershing with a maneuverable re-entry vehicle and radar area-correlation guidance. By comparing the oncoming target with stored images, the missile's accuracy was greatly improved. Compatible with existing Pershing ground equipment, it was still labor intensive, with 3,800 men needed for 108 missiles on launchers.

PREPARATIONS FOR LANCE MISSILE LAUNCH. The Lance was a highly mobile short-to-medium-range surface-to-surface missile system using a self-propelled launcher. It was also the U.S. Army's last nuclear-armed ballistic missile. The missile had a new prepackaged liquid fuel, unlike other army missiles, which gave it a quick reaction time.

LANCE MISSILE LAUNCH, AUGUST 5, 1965. Development began on the Lance in 1962, with flight testing beginning in March 1965. Tests continued through 1977 on a number of different warheads. Immediately upon launch, its four spin motors fired, producing the characteristic black smoke that accompanied every Lance firing.

MULTIPLE LAUNCH ROCKET SYSTEM (MLRS). Another weapon that became synonymous with the 1990–1991 Gulf War, MLSR rockets are solid-fueled with a warhead of bomblets, which earned it the nickname "steel rain." It is a highly mobile surface-to-surface artillery rocket system.

MLSR FIRING. The MLRS launcher is an M270 launcher, essentially a "stretched" Bradley Fighting Vehicle chassis. MLRS began in the mid-1970s as the General Support Rocket System and was fully operational by 1983. The rockets are fired from two pods, each holding six rockets, and can be fired individually or in ripples of 2 to 12.

ARMY TACTICAL MISSILE SYSTEM (ATACMS). Development for ATACMS began in 1982 when the U.S. Army needed a successor for the Lance missile. Its first firing at White Sands was in 1988, and several versions were created, one of which carried 930 M-74 bomblets. Another version employed GPS guidance, while others carried Brilliant anti-tank guided munitions or a 500-pound high explosive warhead.

COPPERHEAD BEING LOADED. In addition to ground and air defense-type weapons, WSMR tests a variety of anti-tank weapons. Here a Copperhead laser-guided munition is being loaded into a towed M198 one hundred fifty-five–millimeter howitzer. The Copperhead was developed in the early 1970s and was fielded in 1982.

COPPERHEAD JUST BEFORE IMPACT. Fired at WSMR's Small Missile Range, the Copperhead had a thermal battery activated upon firing, which spun up a gyroscope. The tailfins popped open, and a laser seeker began scanning for targets. Once the projectile homed in on a target, fins on the middle of the body popped open to guide it in.

LAND LOCKED SHIP 1 (LLS-1), THE DESERT SHIP, AT LAUNCH COMPLEX 34. The U.S. Navy has used this location since the 1940s, and the Desert Ship was completed in 1954 as a way for the navy to test its ship-borne weapons. LLS-1 has the entire infrastructure one would find on an ocean-going vessel with the advantage of being able to recover missiles fired from its launchers.

AEROBEE SOUNDING ROCKET BEING PREPARED FOR LAUNCH. This early photograph shows the rocket without its booster, ready to be loaded into its launch tower. Aerobee was chosen over Viking for the U.S. Navy's sounding rocket program, and thousands of Aerobees were fired by the navy, often on behalf of NASA, in the pursuit of sounding data for upper atmospheric and space research.

AEROBEE 170 LAUNCH. This photograph shows an Aerobee 170 leaving a launcher. Johns Hopkins University's Applied Physics Laboratory was assigned technical direction of the Aerobee project under the direction of Dr. James van Allen. Aerobee was named for Aerojet, the builder of the rocket, and the U.S. Navy's Bumblebee program.

DUAL AEROBEE LAUNCH, NOVEMBER 9, 1971. Aerobee launches were spectacular events, with the rockets leaving their towers, but they sometimes failed. A pamphlet entitled "To the Royal Order of Aerobe Rocketeers," on the history of the program, notes, "Shortly after Jack Heckel became President of Space General, his staff put together a movie of a few spectacular Aerobee blow-ups to be shown at the AIAA Sounding Rocket Conference. After Jack viewed it and expressed his concern about the company image, the film disappeared forever."

AEROBEE ROCKET RECOVERY. Dated July 27, 1976, this photograph's caption states, "View of Aerobee 170 Rocket motor section. S/N NASA 12.033 after impact about two miles northwest of Rhodes Canyon Range Center."

NAVY TYPHON LAUNCH, DECEMBER 17, 1963. The Typhon was to be the last of the U.S. Navy's "T" surface-to-air missiles developed under the Bumblebee project. Essentially a "super Talos," it was to be launched with a solid-fuel booster and powered by a ramjet with Mach 5 capabilities. Many problems plagued the project, however, and it was never fully developed and deployed.

FIRST TALOS LAUNCH AT WSMR, JULY 10, 1951. The Talos was one of three "T" missiles developed from the U.S. Navy's Bumblebee program, begun in 1945 to develop a supersonic, radar-guided, ramjet-propelled missile. Talos used beam-riding guidance, but later semi-active homing was added. It employed an expanding ring-type warhead, which was devastating to airborne targets.

LAST TALOS FIRING, DECEMBER 21, 1972. During its life at White Sands, 528 Talos missiles were fired, giving the missile the most firings for any ever tested here. Talos missiles protected the fleet for 22 years, and after being taken out of service, remaining Talos missiles were renamed Vandal and were used for targets.

POGO-HI BEING PLACED IN LAUNCHER. Developed by New Mexico State University's Physical Sciences Laboratory, Pogo-Hi was a rocket-propelled missile designed primarily for testing missile guidance and control systems. First fired in 1954, the missile was used until 1960 and had a ceiling of 100,000 feet.

TERRIER MISSILE LAUNCH. The Terrier was actually the first of the U.S. Navy's three "T" missiles to enter fleet service. It began as a supersonic test vehicle to evaluate the Talos guidance system. The missile showed promise, so it was developed and put into service while the Talos underwent further development. By 1966, when production ended, more than 8,000 Terriers had been built.

TARTAR MISSILE LAUNCH. The last of the three "T" missiles, the Tartar entered fleet service in the 1960s and was deployed on smaller ships, such as frigates and destroyers, where space for a boosted missile was impractical. Essentially, a Terrier without the booster, the Tartar lasted only a few short years and was replaced by the Standard missile.

TARTAR AND TERRIER ON MK 5 GUIDED MISSILE LAUNCHER. Originally modified and installed at LLS-1 (Desert Ship) in 1977, the MK 5 launcher was used for firing the Standard missile. Shown here with Tartar and Terrier missiles, the MK 5 was the only launcher of its kind and was last used in November 1977. It now resides in the museum's Missile Park.

TERRIER BLACK BRANDT LAUNCH. Black Brandt is a NASA rocket launched by the U.S. Navy at White Sands as a sounding rocket, often carrying instrumentation to measure upper atmosphere heating and solar radiation.

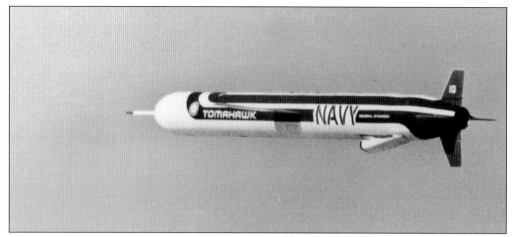

TOMAHAWK MISSILE FLIGHT. The Tomahawk is an all-weather, ship-launched, long-range cruise missile capable of delivering high explosives, bomblets, and even a nuclear warhead. Two hundred eighty-eight Tomahawks were fired during the 1991 Gulf War, bringing into the public conscience this weapon system.

AIR FORCE ATHENA MISSILE, AUGUST 12, 1966. From left to right, U.S. Army colonel Charles Graham (deputy commander of White Sands Missile Range), Utah Secretary of State Clyde Miller, and U.S. Air Force colonel James Caret examine the stabilizer fins of an Athena missile during Miller's tour of the Green River Launch Complex. Colonel Carter was the Athena test conductor at White Sands Missile Range, New Mexico.

ATHENA LAUNCH AT GREEN RIVER, UTAH, JULY 14, 1966. The Athena was a research missile used to test intercontinental ballistic missile re-entry vehicles. During its early years, White Sands had sufficient space for almost any rocket or missile test the United States needed to perform. By the time Athena was developed, the U.S. Army needed on off-range launch site to allow for longer flight distances. Green River, Utah, as well as Fort Wingate, New Mexico, has been used for this purpose.

ATHENA MISSILE BEING PLACED INTO MISSILE PARK. Today Missile Park is part of the White Sands Missile Range Museum. In the past, however, missiles and rockets tested on the range were installed in a triangular-shaped "park" in front of Post Headquarters, shown here.

LITTLE JOE ON LAUNCHER. Developed as part of NASA's Mercury program, Little Joe was designed to replicate the Redstone rocket, which was to be used in the actual program, at a far cheaper cost. Little Joe was an unmanned test capsule built by North American Aviation, with work beginning in 1958.

LITTLE JOE READY FOR FIRING. The Little Joe system was used to test solutions to many of the problems related to early space flight. One of the most important was the need for the crew to escape the booster should anything go wrong during the initial flight of the Mercury-Redstone rocket. A Little Joe can be seen today at the New Mexico Museum of Space History in Alamogordo, New Mexico.

TARGET DRONE FACILITY. This view of a target drone assembly facility shows some two dozen Firebee target drones. There were numerous target facilities across the range, most notably at Launch Complex 32, Orogrande, and Oscura Base Camp.

MATADOR TARGET DRONE. The Matador's first flight was in 1949, and the missile deployed to Bitburg Air Base, Germany, in 1954, armed with a nuclear warhead. By 1962, the cumbersome Matador was removed from service.

MQM 61-A Target Drone. Production of this propeller-driver target drone began in 1959 in response to the U.S. Navy's demand for a gunnery and anti-aircraft target. It could reach speeds of 350 miles per hour, with a ceiling of 43,000 feet, and is no longer in service.

The 61-E Target Drone Launch. This small target drone was one of the earliest flown at the range, and few were fired. This is the only photograph in the museum archives of the aircraft, and there is no further information given. The target, like many, probably did not have a large production.

BEECH CRAFT TARGET DRONE 1025 TJ BEING LAUNCHED. Pictured is the take off of Beech Craft Jet Drone, 1025 TJ, serial number A-460, from "B: Station to be landed at Parker Site, 7 May 64." Two JATO (jet-assisted takeoff) engines on the bottom of the aircraft brought it up to speed so the ramjet engine on the top could then power the target.

MQM 34D MOD II TARGET DRONE. On May 23, 1973, this MQM 34D target drone was launched from B Station. This modification by the Ryan Company included a General Electric J-35 turbojet engine for high acceleration maneuvers.

REDHEAD/ROADRUNNER TARGET ON LAUNCHER, SEPTEMBER 3, 1965. A supersonic target drone first flown in 1961, the Redhead (high altitude) Roadrunner (low altitude) was used at White Sands mainly as a target for testing the Hawk missile system until the mid-1970s.

THE 124-E FIREBEE ARMY TARGET GUIDED MISSILE, JANUARY 30, 1964. The 124 was the second-generation Firebee, with a larger airframe and longer wingspan. It developed about 1,700 pounds of thrust at takeoff and could be either ground or air launched.

NV-123 Drone. On January 31, 1973, Tomas Vazquez records an NV-123 Target Drone. Also called the MQM-7A, this target is guided and has a modified engine to develop greater thrust. Vazquez used a Graflex XL camera with 120 roll film.

MQM-107 Target Drone Launch. The MQM-107 Streaker was a subsonic aerial target developed in the 1970s. It has undergone numerous changes and is still used by the U.S. Army and Air Force.

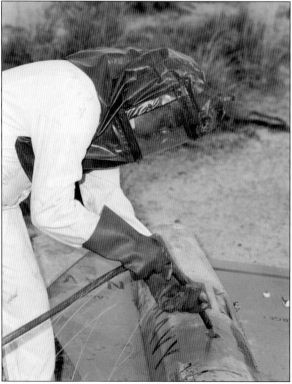

TALOS LAUNCH FROM LSS-1 (DESERT SHIP). At the end of the Talos program, all remaining missiles in the U.S. Navy's inventory were modified and re-designated Vandal targets. Vandal targets could fly from just above ground up to 70,000 feet, and they were often used to simulate in-bound cruise missiles.

WHAT GOES UP, MUST COME DOWN—TARGET DRONE RECOVERY. The reverse of this photograph states, "EOD personnel prepare YAGM-37A for recovery and transport back to White Sands Missile Range headquarters" on May 13, 1976. Most target drones fired at White Sands utilized recovery systems to allow for their reuse.

QF-80 Full-Scale Aerial Target (FSAT). Not all targets used at White Sands were small drone aircraft. When full-sized aircraft were rendered obsolete, they were then often used as targets. One of the first such targets at White Sands was a B-17 Bomber, shot down by a Nike Ajax missile on April 24, 1952. This particular photograph is interesting—there is a pilot in the aircraft, it has the U.S. Air Force emblem on it, yet it has "Navy" painted on it!

PQM-102 FSAT, August 1975. The U.S. Air Force's F-102 was developed into a target in the 1970s. Adaptation for different army user requirements was accomplished by the air force and other White Sands agencies by 1975. Stated on the reverse of the photograph is, "The PQM-102 is a desirable target because of its performance, signature characteristics, and pay-load carrying capabilities."

Vega Target Control Console. FSATs and other aerial targets were flown at White Sands by operators in Range Control Building 300, on White Sands Missile Range's main post, or at King 1, located at Holloman Air Force Base. Launch and recovery control vans launched the targets into the air, and then control was turned over to Vega operators who flew the aircraft in precise patterns on the range. Once the target mission ended, the aircraft was again turned over to the ground control van, which landed the aircraft.

Five

TIME OFF, RECREATION, AND FAMILY LIFE

GILA MONSTERS
1946
HOME GAMES

GILA JUNIOR COLLEGE
THATCHER, ARIZONA

JENNINGS LUMBER COMPANY

— Philco Radios —

SAFFORD 278 - 279   PIMA 10

GAME FLYER FROM GILA JUNIOR COLLEGE MONSTERS, 1946. Listed in the flyer are coaches and team members. WSPG was led by coach Capt. Frederick Spann, U.S. Military Academy; assistant coaches were Capt. Altus Prince, U.S. Military Academy; Lt. Donald Franklin, Creighton University; and Lt. Richard Jones, University of Kentucky.

FOOTBALL TEAM, 1947, WHITE SANDS PROVING GROUND. WSPG fielded many sports teams; because of its relative isolation, they were always popular and had great support post-wide. Identified only by last name, from left to right, are Grernomo, Harris, Overton, Phoffier, Clark, Reatle, and Wiess.

LOS ALAMOS FOOTBALL TEAM, 1947. The football team is at Los Alamos, New Mexico, playing against the A-Bombs in November 1947. Identified by jersey number and last name are 31–Kistner, 43–Riskie, 52–Insley, 45–Henrich, 24–Hemmrold, and 53–Overton.

FOOTBALL GAME FLYER. The flyer reads, "White Sands Skybusters Versus the Roswell Army Airfield Atomic Bombers." By the time of its closure in 1967, Roswell Army Airfield, later Walker Air Force Base, was the largest Strategic Air Command base in the United States. After returning from Tinian and its mission to drop the atomic bombs on Japan, the 509th Bombardment Group made Roswell its home, hence the 509th on the flyer.

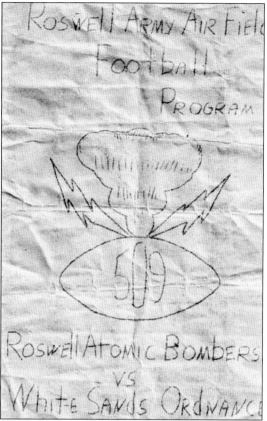

SOFTBALL GAME AT WSPG. While fall and winter provided football to those stationed at WSPG, spring and summer meant softball, with both army and navy teams playing regular games on what later became Goddard Field, which is just west, across Headquarters Avenue, from the WSMR museum.

ENLISTED CLUB. For those evenings where there were no sports to take in, many enlisted members of White Sands retired to the Enlisted Members' (EM) Club after a day of shooting missiles. The club now houses the offices of Army Community Services.

OFFICERS' CLUB BAR, 1953. The Officers' Club was eventually moved to a new location near the officers' housing area, and the old club was turned over to Public Affairs. The building housed their offices and a small museum until recently, when Public Affairs moved into another building. The Officers' Club still sits empty and forlorn, awaiting a new tenant.

Sierra Chapel, WSMR, January 18, 1971. The Sierra Chapel was a World War II temporary building that was moved onto the post to house the first religious services. It is used today for Catholic Mass.

Post Library, 1956. For those with more intellectual pursuits, sports and the clubs could be forsaken for the post library. Librarians Mary Miller (left) and Margaret Zinich (right) are identified in this photograph. In addition to the post library, a separate technical library was maintained and available to scientists and engineers at the post.

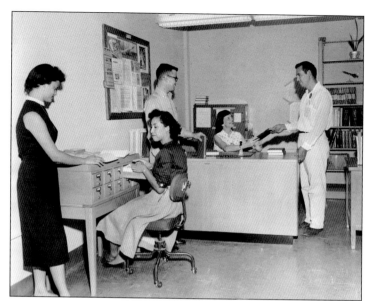

POST LIBRARY, SEPTEMBER 14, 1956. Patrons look through the card catalog and check out books from the library. Of particular note is the size of the card catalog—only 10 card drawers. The library was quite small in the early days. Identified in this photograph are Nettie Engram (seated) and Emila Sutton (looking through the catalog).

CLYDE TOMBAUGH AT A WHITE SANDS NATIONAL MONUMENT PICNIC. A handwritten caption for this photograph states, "An informal picnic at the W. S. Monument. Pictured from left to right are M/SGT Bill Dennison (now residing in Albuquerque, NM), W. O. Ralph Gonzales (now residing in San Jose, CA.) CPL Clayton, Mrs. J Showberg, Doris Brunelle (living with me for 52 years), and Clyde Tombaugh (standing). Besides working with Clyde on many photograph projects we were neighbors in Las Cruces. I often spent time in his backyard gazing at the heavens on his telescope."

THANKSGIVING MEAL. This 1950 photograph depicts members of I Battery having dinner at the mess hall. Pictured are Marice Gonzales, battery commander Captain Ball, William Dennison, Edward May, Maurice Brunelle, D. Walker, and Mrs. Ball. The two boys are sons of Captain and Mrs. Ball.

WOMEN'S CLUB ANNUAL DINNER DANCE, JUNE 2, 1956. By 1953, there were a number of women's clubs being formed at WSPG, the first of which was simply the Women's Club. As the population of the post grew, clubs specifically for the spouses of officers, noncommissioned officers (NCOs), and enlisted members were formed. Formal dinners, teas, and other events helped break the monotony of living in isolation.

NCO Auxiliary Tea, September 16, 1956. Formal teas such as this one were an important part of the cycle of events for the women's clubs at White Sands Proving Ground. The tea set itself can be seen in the WSMR museum.

State Luncheon. On November 12, 1958, the Women's Club presented a "State Luncheon." Here members Mrs. A. B. Haas, Mrs. R. D. Skelton, Mrs. R. W. Elliot, Mrs. C. E. Schwitters, and Mrs. F. A. Wood present a skit.

U.S. WIVES MISSILE, PART OF THE NOVEMBER 12, 1958, STATE LUNCHEON. This particular missile, developed by the Women's Club and examined here by Mrs. W. C. Fuller, utilized a unique propulsion system, seen here at the base of the missile.

WINNING HATS. During the November 1958 State Luncheon, there was also a hat competition, with the winners shown here. Mrs. R. V. Buebe models the winning hat for the state of Texas, with Mrs. J. P. McGovern modeling the tobacco leaf hat for "Carolina."

FASHION SHOW PREP, MARCH 11, 1958. Other popular activities put on by the women's clubs were the annual spring and fall fashion shows. These events brought the entire family in, as shown here by Susan Wark and Kenneth Fowler practicing their posture and curtsies.

EASTER HAT SHOW. Children were not the only ones to become involved in activities of the Women's Club. Majors F. W. Scott and E. J. Miltenberger, with Capt. L. N. Newberry and Col. Howard Coleman, model hats for the Spring Easter Hat Show in March 1956.

BIRTHDAY LUNCHEON. The January 15, 1958, Birthday Luncheon featured Mrs. J. W. Shere, Mrs. P. W. Leslie, and Mrs. R. E. Skelton posed in their favorite fur wraps, hats, and gloves.

COFFEE CHAT. A handwritten note on the club scrapbook states, "Talking over club plans for the New Year are these three members of the White Sands Woman's Club which launched its 1957–58 year with a coffee hour Tuesday morning honoring the club's new members. From left are Mrs. R. H. Wise, new member; Mrs. Robert Mackintosh, daughter of Maj. Gen. W. E. Laidlaw, WSPG Commander, and Mrs. John Seddon."

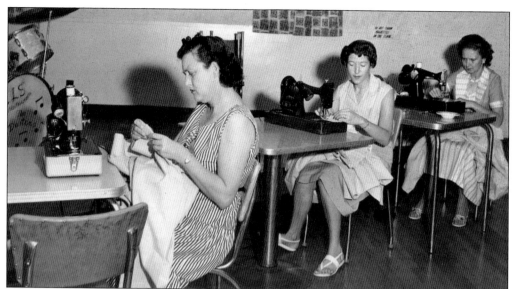

SEWING CLASS. The women's clubs offered more than just luncheons and teas. Classes such as cooking, wine tasting, and, as seen here, sewing were offered throughout the year.

VISITORS TO THE RANGE, OCTOBER 22, 1958. White Sands women's clubs hosted local clubs, bringing them in to visit the range. Here are, from left to right, Mrs. W. H. Clifford of White Sands; Mrs. Asbury Glover, vice president of the Alamogordo Women's Club; Mrs. Ira Faney, of the Women's Improvement Association in Las Cruces; and Mrs. D. H. McCune of the El Paso Woman's Club.

OUT FOR A RIDE. Horseback riding was a popular pastime in the 1950s and 1960s. This photograph, dated December 5, 1957, shows, from left to right, Inga and Carl Young, Bob and Lois Mackintosh, and "Tex" and Shirley Penney.

WHITE SANDS PROVING GROUND. Jack Benny and Ann Blyth are shown atop a WAC Corporal. Benny and Blythe visited White Sands Proving Ground as part of a USO tour during the Christmas season of 1951.

ARRIVAL OF PRES. JOHN F. KENNEDY, JUNE 5, 1963. The visit of President Kennedy was much anticipated at WSMR and provided the range's population the opportunity to see the president up close. The event was called Project MEWS, for Missile Exercise White Sands.

KENNEDY SPEAKING. The president addressed the crowd before viewing missile launches. The president arrived at Holloman Air Force Base and was then flown to White Sands to visit two of the launch complexes.

THE ROPE LINE—SHAKING HANDS BEFORE GOING TO VIEW LAUNCHES. The first stop was to view an Honest John firing, where the briefer had two minutes to explain the capabilities of the missile and its preparations. It was then fired at a hillside downrange. A Little John, Sergeant, and Hawk were then fired.

123

WATCHING A LAUNCH. The party then moved to Launch Complex 37, where a Nike Hercules was launched against another Nike Hercules. They also watched a Nike Zeus firing and a navy Talos firing against an F-80 jet.

REVIEWING THE TROOPS. Before leaving White Sands, the president had the opportunity to meet and review the troops from White Sands, Fort Bliss, and Fort Sill, Oklahoma. He departed after a visit of only two and a half hours and is still the only president to visit White Sands while in office.

WAITING FOR COLUMBIA. Because of weather problems at Edwards Air Force Base in California, the decision was made by NASA to land the orbiter Columbia at WSMR's Northrup Strip, near White Sands National Monument, and public viewing stands were erected. Thousands of people showed up to watch the landing.

SPACE SHUTTLE APPROACHING. Because of the ferocious windstorm on March 29, Columbia orbited for another day, landing at WSMR on March 30, 1982. Here the shuttle is approaching and is only seconds from touchdown.

TOUCHDOWN. Landing at 9:05 a.m. Mountain Standard Time, STS-3, the shuttle's third orbital test flight, brought Comdr. Jack Lousma and pilot C. Gordon Fullerton to White Sands. A crowd of thousands cheered the landing.

GETTING READY TO GO. The stiff-legged Derrick hoists the orbiter onto the back of a 747 for its ride back to Florida. NASA had to move 350 people and two trains of equipment from Edwards Air Force Base to White Sands, and after only seven days, in which some 90,000 people viewed the shuttle, the orbiter was on its way home.

HERMANN OBERTH VISITS WHITE SANDS MISSILE RANGE, MAY 24, 1982. On this date, the range hosted an extraordinary visitor: Hermann Oberth (far right), Werner von Braun's mentor and an early proponent of rocketry. Shaking hands with Oberth is Col. Dan Duggan.

BIBLIOGRAPHY

Boehm, William B. *From Barren Desert to Thriving Community: A Social History of White Sands Missile Range, 1945–1954.* WSMR Archeological Research Report No. 97-14, 1997.

Gunston, Bill. *The Illustrated Encyclopedia of the World's Rockets and Missiles.* New York: Crescent Books, 1979.

Kelly, Cynthia C., ed. *The Manhattan Project: The Birth of the Atomic Bomb in the Words of Its Creators, Eyewitnesses, and Historians.* New York: Black Dog and Leventhal Publishers, 2007.

Kleem, Ernst, and Otto Merk. *The Birth of the Missile, The Secrets of Peenemunde.* New York: E. P. Dutton and Company, 1965.

Lamont, Lansing. *Day of Trinity.* New York: Atheneum, 1965.

Merlan, Thomas. *Life at Trinity Base Camp.* WSMR Archeological Research Report No. 01-07, 2001.

Morgan, Mark L., and Mark A. Berhow. *Rings of Supersonic Steel: Air Defenses of the United States Army, 1950–1979.* San Pedro, CA: Fort MacArthur Press, 2002.

Neufeld, Michael J. *The Rocket and the Reich: Peenemunde and the Coming of the Ballistic Missile Era.* New York: The Free Press, 1995.

Ordway, Frederick I., and Mitchell Sharpe. *The Rocket Team, From the V-2 to the Saturn Moon Rocket—the Inside Story of How a Small Group of Engineers Changed World History.* New York: Thomas Y. Crowell Publishers, 1975.

Pretty, Ronald, ed. *Jane's Pocket Book of Missiles.* New York: Collier Books, 1975.

Rhodes, Richard. *The Making of the Atomic Bomb.* New York: Simon and Shuster, 1986.

Siuru, Bill. *Planes Without Pilots.* Blue Ridge Summit, PA: TAB Books, 1991.

Szasz, Ferenc Morton. *The Day the Sun Rose Twice: The Story of the Trinity Site Nuclear Explosion July 16, 1945.* Albuquerque: University of New Mexico Press, 1984.

Ulanoff, Stanley. *Illustrated Guide to U.S. Missiles and Rockets.* Garden City, NY: Doubleday and Company, 1959.

White Sands History, Range Beginnings and Early Missile Testing. White Sands Missile Range Public Affairs Office. Unpublished reprint of a 1959 WSMR Historical Report.

ACROSS AMERICA, PEOPLE ARE DISCOVERING
SOMETHING WONDERFUL. *THEIR HERITAGE.*

Arcadia Publishing is the leading local history publisher in the United States. With more than 4,000 titles in print and hundreds of new titles released every year, Arcadia has extensive specialized experience chronicling the history of communities and celebrating America's hidden stories, bringing to life the people, places, and events from the past. To discover the history of other communities across the nation, please visit:

www.arcadiapublishing.com

Customized search tools allow you to find regional history books about the town where you grew up, the cities where your friends and family live, the town where your parents met, or even that retirement spot you've been dreaming about.